I0068081

WordTOOLS

For

Business

Vol. 1

Harnessing the
Power of Words!

Carol L Rickard, LCSW

Well YOUniversity® Publications

Sign up now!

To be sure to get our weekly motivational &

inspirational quotes and stories!

ThePowerOfWordsEQuote.com

Copyright © 2017 Carol L. Rickard

All Licensing by Well YOUniversity, LLC

All rights reserved.

ISBN-13: 978-1947745025

WordTools for Business Vol. 1

Harnessing the Power of Words!

by Carol L Rickard, LCSW

© Copyright 2015 Well YOUniversity Publications

ISBN 13: 978-1947745025

All rights reserved.

No part of this book may be reproduced for resale, redistribution, or any other purposes (including but not limited to eBooks, pamphlets, articles, video or audiotapes, & handouts or slides for lectures or workshops).

Licenses to reproduce these materials for those and any other purposes must be obtained from the author and Well YOUniversity.

WellYOUniversity®
RESTORING HOPE, HEALTH, AND HAPPINESS

888 LIFE TOOLS (543-3866)

Carol@WellYOUniversity.com

Welcome!

My 1st WordTool came to me in 2006 when doing a group with my patients. How could I get them to *welcome* change in their lives?

Creating **H**ealthy **A**nd **N**ew **G**rowth **E**xperiences!

From there it's been an onward journey! Most of them are inspired by persons or situations. My hope is to create Ah-Ah moments that can help change a life!

They are officially called "Artinyms", which is Sanskrit for "describe".

On the back of each wordtool is a question for you. Answering them will serve to strengthen your business & lead to more success!.

~To Living Well TODAY! ~

Carol

Sign up now!

To be sure to get our weekly motivational & inspirational quotes and stories!

ThePowerOfWordsEQuote.com

A
Conscious
Choice
Enabling
Powerful
Transformation

COPYRIGHT 2017 & Licensed by Well YOUniversity, LLC

What are you are having difficulty accepting that could be holding you back?

A

Critical

Task

Implemented

Only

Now!

COPYRIGHT 2017 & Licensed by Well YOUniversity, LLC

What actions do you need to take in order to have more success?

Awareness

Towards

Thoughts &

Emotions

Needed

To

Improve

Our

Nature

COPYRIGHT 2017 & Licensed by Well YOUniversity, LLC

Are there any areas that you need to be paying closer attention to?

A

Variation

Only

Increasing

Difficulties

And

Negative

Consequences

Everytime!

COPYRIGHT 2017 & Licensed by Well YOUniversity, LLC

In what ways do you tend to avoid?
What is something you have been avoiding?

Become

Lost

Amongst

Many

Excuses

COPYRIGHT 2017 & Licensed by Well YOUniversity, LLC

When was the last time you blamed someone or something instead of owning responsibility?

Cultivating

A

Responsive

Environment

COPYRIGHT 2017 & Licensed by Well YOUniversity, LLC

In what ways can you improve on your environment and make it more caring?

Constantly

Having

Activity

Obstruct

Success!

COPYRIGHT 2017 & Licensed by Well YOUniversity, LLC

What is the chaos you need to remove from your
life in order to have success?

Concentrate

On

Making

Problems

Larger

Actually

Increasing

Negativity

COPYRIGHT 2017 & Licensed by Well YOUniversity, LLC

Make a list of all the things you have been
complaining about:

Challenge

Ourselves

Make

Matters

Important

Today!

COPYRIGHT 2017 & Licensed by Well YOUniversity, LLC

What do you need to commit to that has been difficult for you to do?

Deciding

I

Stay

Committed

In

Purpose

Letting

In

No

Excuse!

COPYRIGHT 2017 & Licensed by Well YOUniversity, LLC

What are some areas where you need to be a little more disciplined?

Denied

Opportunity

Not

'

Trying!

COPYRIGHT 2017 & Licensed by Well YOUniversity, LLC

What have been some instances when you have stopped yourself by not even trying?

Daringly

Recognize

Experiences

As

Mine

COPYRIGHT 2017 & Licensed by Well YOUniversity, LLC

What are some of your dreams?

Educate &

Motivate

People

On

Ways

Excel

Repeatedly

COPYRIGHT 2017 & Licensed by Well YOUniversity, LLC

Who is someone you have empowered?

What did you do?

Engage

Xternal

Circumstances

Undermining

Self

Empowerment

COPYRIGHT 2017 & Licensed by Well YOUniversity, LLC

What is the last excuse you made?

What was the real reason?

Face

An

Important

Lesson

COPYRIGHT 2017 & Licensed by Well YOUniversity, LLC

What are some of the important lessons you have
learned the hard way?

Focus

In

Now

Instead

Stopping

Halfway

COPYRIGHT 2017 & Licensed by Well YOUniversity, LLC

Make a list of all the things you have not finished.
Do each one & cross it off the list once done!

Get

Our

Activity

Lined-up

Straight

COPYRIGHT 2017 & Licensed by Well YOUniversity, LLC

What are some of the goals you have for yourself
in the next 6 months? Year?

Giving

Respect

And

Thanks

Into

The

Usual

Daily

Experiences

COPYRIGHT 2017 & Licensed by Well YOUniversity, LLC

Make a list of all the things you hold gratitude
towards in your life:

Having

A

Behavior

Internally

Triggered

COPYRIGHT 2017 & Licensed by Well YOUniversity, LLC

What habits do you need to get rid of?

What new habits do you need to establish?

I

Make

Powerful

Adjustments

Concerning

Today

COPYRIGHT 2017 & Licensed by Well YOUniversity, LLC

What is one way you can have a lasting impact
on the world?

Look &

Establish

A

Direction

Enabling

Real

Success

COPYRIGHT 2017 & Licensed by Well YOUniversity, LLC

Who have been some of your best leaders?
What made them so good?

Living

Intentionally &

Fully

Engaged

COPYRIGHT 2017 & Licensed by Well YOUniversity, LLC

What does you "best life" look like?

Making

Incremental

Steps

Towards

Achieving

Key

Efforts

COPYRIGHT 2017 & Licensed by Well YOUniversity, LLC

What are some of the mistakes you've made
where you have learned the most?

Natural

Opportunity

To

Inspect

Current

Experiences

COPYRIGHT 2017 & Licensed by Well YOUniversity, LLC

When was the last time you took time to notice
the wonderful things around you?

Purposely

Repeat

Activities

Critical

To

Improving

Core

Elements

COPYRIGHT 2017 & Licensed by Well YOUniversity, LLC

What are some skills that if you were to practice more often could really change your life?

Powerful

Underlying

Reason

Push

Ourselves

Stretch

Everyday!

COPYRIGHT 2017 & Licensed by Well YOUniversity, LLC

What are the reasons you push yourself to stretch everyday?

Re-examine

Experiences

For

Lessons

Enabling

Corrections

Today

COPYRIGHT 2017 & Licensed by Well YOUniversity, LLC

What have been some of the greatest lessons
you have learned from past experiences?

See

Everyone

Receives

Valuable

Experience

COPYRIGHT 2017 & Licensed by Well YOUniversity, LLC

What are some ways or actions you can take to improve on your service?

Together

Embrace

A

Mission

COPYRIGHT 2017 & Licensed by Well YOUniversity, LLC

What has been one of your most rewarding team experiences so far?

Take

Responsibility

Until

Totally

Honest

COPYRIGHT 2017 & Licensed by Well YOUniversity, LLC

When was the last time you didn't tell the truth
and why not?

About the Author

Carol L Rickard, LCSW, TTS, of Hopewell, NJ is founder & CEO of WellYOUniversity, LLC, a global health education company dedicated *to empowering individuals with the tools and supports to achieve lifelong wellness & recovery.*

Also known as **America's Wellness Ambassador**, Carol is a dynamic & engaging speaker who brings to life practical / useful solutions. She is a weekly contributor for Esperanza Magazine; written 13 books on stress and wellness, had a guest appearance on Dr. Oz last year

She is also the creator & host of a 30-minute wellness show on Princeton TV - **The WELL YOU Show** which current episodes are aired on Mondays at 6:00pm EST & Sundays at 8:30am EST and can be watched at PrincetonTV.org.

All episodes available at: **www.TheWELLYOUShow.com**

Get more of Carol at:

Twitter: **@wellYOUlife**

"Like us" @ www.FaceBook.com/WellYOUniversity

Have Carol Speak at Your Next Event!

Get more information about how you can have Carol speak at your organization, event, or conference.

Go to: www.CarolLRickard.com

Or call: 888 Life Tools (543-3866)

Carol's Other Books

Getting Your Mind to Mind You

ANGER – A Simple & Practical Approach

Help – How to Help Those Who DON'T Want it

Selfness – Simple Self-Care Secrets

Stress Eating – How to STOP Using Food to Cope

Stretched Not Broken – Caregiver's Stress

The Caregiver's Toolbox

Transforming Illness to Wellness

Putting Your Weight Loss on Auto

The Benefits of Smoking

Moving Beyond Depression

LifeTools – How to Manage Life

Creating Compliance

Relapse Prevention

Please visit us at:

www.WellYOUniversity.com

Sign up for weekly motivational e-quote!

Check out our upcoming FREE webinars!

Learn more about our training programs.

WellYOUniversity®
RESTORING HOPE, HEALTH, AND HAPPINESS

Email us your success story at:

Success@WellYOUniversity.com

We'd like to ask for your feedback

Please check out the next page
if this book has been HELPFUL for you!

We'd love to hear from you!

Feedback Card

Please take a moment & provide us some

feedback about the book you just read &

how you feel *it benefited YOU!*

_____

_____

_____

_____

Name: _____

Best Phone #: _____

Can we use your comments in our publicity materials?

Yes / No

If OK with you, what's the best time to call you:_____

Thank You!

Scan or take a picture & email:

Carol@WellYOUniversity.com

Snail mail: Carol Rickard

5 Zion Rd., Hopewell, NJ 08535

Tear along here

www.ingramcontent.com/pod-product-compliance
Lightning Source LLC
Chambersburg PA
CBHW070859210326
41521CB00010B/2010

9781947745025